Original title:
Sassafras Soliloquies

Copyright © 2025 Creative Arts Management OÜ
All rights reserved.

Author: Milo Harrington
ISBN HARDBACK: 978-1-80567-251-7
ISBN PAPERBACK: 978-1-80567-550-1

Dialogue with Dappled Sunlight

Dancing shadows on the ground,
They whisper secrets, all around.
Sunshine chuckles through the trees,
A game of hide and seek with ease.

Branches wave, a leafy cheer,
Nature's laughter drifts so near.
Bright rays tease and play along,
Who knew sunlight could be strong?

Sylvan Serenades in Silhouette

A squirrel prances, tail held high,
While birds in chorus learn to fly.
Mice practice their tap dance, too,
As shadows play the lead in view.

The moonlight giggles, stars applaud,
While owls hoot a night-time nod.
Branches sway in gentle breeze,
Nature's rhythm puts us at ease.

When the Earth Speaks Softly

Mossy carpets, nature's stage,
Earth's soft whispers beyond this age.
With every rustle, tales unfold,
Of merry critters, brave and bold.

The ground chuckles as we trot,
Telling us secrets that it forgot.
Beneath our feet, the stories flow,
In humor's grasp, they love to grow.

Echoes from the Heartwood

Trees gossip low with creaking sound,
While beetles march in outfits brown.
The roots giggle under soil,
A party's brewing, what a spoil!

Leaves rustle jokes of days gone past,
As breezes swirl and dance so fast.
Echoes bounce among the trunks,
A woodland giggle that never shrinks.

Enchanted Leaves and Lost Dreams

In the woods where giggles play,
Mischief bounces every day.
Leaves whisper tales of jests untold,
In patches of sunlight, secrets unfold.

A squirrel dons a tiny hat,
Singing to an unsuspecting cat.
Dreams of acorns fill the air,
As laughter dances everywhere.

Mushrooms giggle, oh what a sight,
In this mystical woodland light.
With every twist, a new surprise,
Nature's humor beneath blue skies.

Branches sway with glee and flair,
Tickling noses, wild and bare.
In the realms of green delight,
Lost dreams sprout, taking flight.

Musings Under the Canopy

Under branches, tales collide,
Beneath the leaves, where dreams abide.
A bunny hops, wearing a frown,
While squirrels steal nuts from the town.

Clouds drift by with cheeky grins,
Poking fun at nature's sins.
The sun wears shades, quite full of sass,
As the wise old owl gives each a pass.

A brook babbles jokes so clear,
Sharing laughs for all to hear.
Every ripple, a playful tease,
Woven into the charming breeze.

Shadows dance with playful glee,
As leaves sing tunes of jubilee.
Every step on this woodland show,
Takes us where wild wonders grow.

The Secrets of Forest Floors

Creeping critters, fast and sly,
Reveal the secrets they can't deny.
With tiny boots, they stomp and play,
In a dance where mischief lays.

Mossy carpets underneath,
Harboring laughter, holding teeth.
A rabbit giggles, losing track,
As a hedgehog rolls, with sass intact.

Whispers swirl, a breeze so light,
Tales of shenanigans in the night.
Footsteps soft, like clouds they tread,
Imagine what the mushrooms said!

A leaf parade, hats made of gold,
Invitations to antics unfold.
In this realm so wild and free,
Secrets tumble, filled with glee.

Leafy Confessions at Dusk

As twilight falls, the leaves engage,
Sharing tales from a secret stage.
They gossip softly, like a breeze,
Tickling cheeks with playful tease.

A woodpecker strikes a silly pose,
While a raccoon tells jokes no one knows.
The moon giggles, casting a glow,
As whispers mingle with shadows below.

Nature's choir sings off-key,
With croaks and chirps, such harmony.
In every nook, laughter shall bloom,
Under the blush of nature's room.

With every dusk, a chance to share,
Leafy confessions float through the air.
In this woodland, pure delight,
Funny moments take their flight.

Conversations with Eucalyptus Shadows

In the grove where whispers dwell,
The shadows chat, oh what a spell!
One says, "Hey, I lost my leaf!"
The other laughs, "That's just your grief!"

They gossip 'bout the sunny day,
And how the clouds just float away.
"Did you see that silly bug?"
"It danced like it was on a rug!"

Beneath the Whispering Boughs

Under boughs that twist and sway,
The branches giggle, come what may.
"Did you hear what Oak just said?"
"He thinks the wind will scratch his head!"

A squirrel jumps, adds to the tease,
"You all know I'm the one who frees!"
But the branches chuckle with delight,
As nuts rain down in friendly fight!

The Riddle of Roots and Rain

In the depths, the roots unwind,
They ponder life, oh how they're blind!
"What's green and grows with every shower?"
"That's easy, my friend, it's a flower!"

Then Rain chimed in with a splash,
"I'm the star of this leafy bash!"
The roots all giggled, as seeds took hold,
While stories of storms began to unfold!

Chants of the Verdant Spirits

Up in the canopies, spirits sing,
They croon about the joys of spring.
"What's the secret of a leaf's bright hue?"
"It's all in the sunlight, and a sprinkle or two!"

They sway like dancers, in the breeze,
"Shall we tell stories? Oh please, oh please!"
With laughter bubbling under the sun,
They chant till day's end, a whimsical run!

Whimsies of the Wandering Wind

The wind danced by with a cheeky grin,
Waving at leaves in a playful spin.
"Catch me if you can!" it teased the trees,
Tickling the branches, such bold, carefree breeze.

A squirrel laughed loud, wearing acorn hats,
Chasing behind, with some twists and sprats.
"Oh, you think you're fast? Just take a seat!"
The wind looped back, trying to cheat.

Clouds joined the game, drifting in style,
Puffing their cheeks, wearing fluff for a mile.
"We're the observants of this grand parade!"
As giggles and breezes made jokes in the glade.

Then night came along with a ticklish breeze,
Serenading the stars with whimsical tease.
In the moonlight's glow, they all gathered 'round,
For laughs and for jokes, where fun knows no bounds.

Elysium of Echoing Eucalyptus

In a grove of trees, where the laughter flows,
Eucalyptus whispers, and the tale grows.
"Have you seen the owl with the silly hue?"
Dancing on branches, he hoots just for you.

The koalas chuckle, munching their leaves,
Making puns about how no one believes.
"It's never too late for a eucalyptus feast!"
With giggling done, they invited the beast.

A wallaby bounced in, wearing socks of blue,
"I lost them in a race, do you have a clue?"
The trees all chuckled, their laughter so sweet,
As the forest echoed with every heartbeat.

With twilight approaching, the fun carried on,
Breezes played tunes under the dusk's dawn.
The night, softly filled with chuckles and cheer,
In this echoing space, it's all joy, never fear.

Chronicles of Bark and Breeze

Once a tree spoke with a leaf,
Sharing secrets, what a relief!
"Your gossip's green, but still quite sweet,"
Chirped the breeze, swirling with a beat.

A squirrel listened, eyes quite wide,
As witty whispers filled the tide.
"You think you're funny, but you're just bark,"
Came a retort from a nearby park.

Underneath the sun's bright glare,
The branches danced without a care.
"Oh, let's poke fun at the old oak,"
Laughed the wind, it's quite the joke!

In this wood, we jest and play,
A symphony of green ballet.
Bark and breeze in their own rhyme,
Tickling woes of endless time.

The Silence Between the Saplings

In a hush where the young trees sway,
A tiny bird fluffs in a cheeky way.
"Does anyone think two trunks look great?"
Cawed the crow, sealing their fate.

Saplings giggle as shadows boast,
About the tallest, an ancient ghost.
"Who needs height when you're so spry?"
Chortled the grass, just passing by.

Whispers strummed along the roots,
Of fables hidden in old boots.
"Hey you, junior, how's it feel?"
Asked a rock, all covered in teal.

Between saplings, jokes do bloom,
A festival of green, no gloom.
Nature's laughter fills the air,
In a world where trees just don't care.

Impressions of Iridescent Insects

Buzzing thoughts on wings so bright,
Insects flaunt their colorful flight.
"Do I look like a disco ball?"
Said a beetle, trying not to fall.

Caterpillars munching in style,
Smile wide, it's all worthwhile.
"A diet of leaves is just so chic,"
Chimed a ladybug, trying to speak.

A spider spun jokes in her web,
Enticing all to join her ebb.
"Life's not simple, but it's so grand,"
As she tickled the bugs, brood in hand.

With whimsy marking every fill,
Nature's creatures dance at will.
In the light, they take their stance,
Where laughter lingers, life's a dance.

The Tapestry of Twigs and Time

Twigs entwined with stories old,
They hold secrets and wonders untold.
"Here lies a nest with dreams anew,"
Said the fern to the morning dew.

Time ticked softly on the bark,
The herbs rejoiced, each tiny spark.
"If twigs could talk, oh what they'd say,"
Snickered the rock, in disarray.

Lacy shadows danced on ground,
Roots conspiring all around.
"We're just the backdrop, don't you see?"
Whispered the leaves, light and free.

In this realm of twisty rhyme,
Every crack presents a climb.
Life's fabric's woven, rich and bright,
Under the stars, all feels just right.

Tales of Twilight's Tenderness

Under the fading sun's embrace,
Bunnies dance with perfect grace.
A squirrel tells a cheesy joke,
While shadows plot, and moonbeams poke.

Fireflies twinkle like tiny stars,
While frogs croak tales of wild bazars.
Each laugh echoes through the night,
As crickets join in with delight.

Philosophies from the Phosphorescent Paths

Wandering by the glowing trees,
I ponder life, and crack a tease.
Why do owls wear glasses, friend?
To read the tales that never end?

The path shines bright, like disco lights,
As raccoons throw their wild delights.
They debate the best hat styles,
While fireflies turn up with their miles.

Meditations in the Mystic Green

In the meadow, giggles rise,
As hedgehogs wear their funny ties.
A rabbit worth his weight in carrots,
Tells stories that no one inherits.

Laughter echoes through the grass,
Where mushrooms grow, and time does pass.
A dance with daisies, wild and free,
Reminds us all to just be silly.

Observations of the Overarching Branch

Under branches, wise and grand,
Chickens gossip, close at hand.
Why did the bird cross the way?
To prove it wasn't just a play.

With leaves that whisper all around,
And acorns plop upon the ground.
Squirrels debate the best nut stash,
As laughter fills the air with a splash.

Revelations from the Resting Roots

In the garden, secrets hum,
The worms debate, 'Who's more fun?'
Rabbits gossip, tails in a twist,
While daisies dance, who can resist?

A beetle brags about his might,
'I've seen the world from morning light!'
The ants march on in perfect line,
While leaves just giggle, looking fine.

Flowers claim they smell the best,
They argue loudly, none can rest!
Sunlight spills in playful glee,
What a riot, come watch and see!

So rest your roots, take a chance,
Join the fun, it's time to dance!
Nature's jesters gather 'round,
In the whispers, joy is found.

Melodies of the Misty Meadow

In the misty dawn, frogs start to croak,
Each tiny note, a humorous joke.
Crickets chirp with rhythmic flair,
'These grass blades? We're styling our hair!'

The butterflies flaunt their vibrant wings,
Sipping nectar and sharing flings.
While daisies applaud in blooming cheer,
'The more you swirl, the more we leer!'

A bumblebee with swagger flies,
'Buzzing's great, but have you tried fries?'
Marsh insects hitch a melody ride,
Their laughter echoes, can't be denied!

Misty meadows filled with laughter,
Life's a song, joy follows after.
Join the spree, don't miss the cue,
In nature's choir, there's room for you!

Cascades of Color and Sound

Colors tumble—yellow and red,
Leaves swirl around like a dancer's thread.
The wind whispers jokes about the bugs,
While puddles reflect the world's funny hugs.

Splashing raindrops add to the mix,
Nature's rhythm, a playful fix.
Mud pies crafted with laughter and cheer,
'Just watch your step, we're muddy here!'

A riot of hues in the light's soft embrace,
Each blossom giggles, has its own grace.
As sounds intertwine in a joyful spell,
Even the rocks have stories to tell.

From high above, the skybirds jest,
Life's a party—call it the best!
Cascades of joy, let the colors flow,
In this wild fiesta, dance and glow!

The Breath of Blossoms

Blossoms chatter in the bright sunshine,
'Look at us, we're simply divine!'
Petals prance, with fragrance to spill,
A bumblebee dares to take his thrill.

'What's that? A snail? Let's start a race!'
The daisies giggle, 'He'll lose his pace!'
With every gust, all sway and move,
Nature's rhythm, the dance will improve.

A squirrel hops in, quick as a thought,
Stealing seeds from the very spot.
Lilacs shout, 'Stop that little thief!'
As laughter ensues, too grand to be brief!

Breath of blossoms, so crisp, so bright,
In this wild joke, everything feels right.
So come on down, smell the fresh air,
Join our laughter, if you dare!

Laughter of the Hidden Glens

In the glens where giggles play,
Little critters dance all day.
Squirrels juggling acorns high,
While the rabbits laugh and sigh.

Leaves rustle with a cheeky cheer,
As the frogs croak jokes quite clear.
Bumblebees buzz with glee aloud,
Creating quite the silly crowd.

A raccoon in a hat so neat,
Claims he's king of this fine street.
With a wink and a playful grin,
He flips and flops and enters in.

So come and join this merry throng,
Where the laughter is never wrong.
In hidden glens, the joy runs free,
With whimsy wrapped in mystery.

Whims of Whistlewood Winds

In Whistlewood where breezes tease,
The trees sway as if to please.
A gusty giggle tickles leaves,
While mischief sparks and never leaves.

Winds whip around with playful swirls,
As dandelion fluff twirls and twirls.
A butterfly in disguise plays coy,
Chasing shadows with pure joy.

The whispers turn to laughter bright,
As crickets strum in the fading light.
A fox in socks joins the fun,
Dancing until the day is done.

So listen close to nature's rhyme,
As winds conspire to steal your time.
In Whistlewood, the chuckles soar,
Promising smiles forevermore.

Whispers of the Winding Woods

In winding woods where secrets dwell,
The trees gossip; they know it well.
A chipmunk's tale of hidden snacks,
Leaves all the critters giggling in packs.

Underfoot, the mushrooms dance,
They're in a quirky, funny trance.
Each path leads to a new surprise,
With squirrels acting like wiseguys.

Soft whispers float on the breeze,
As the woodpecker cracks jokes with ease.
Frolicsome fawns jump up and down,
In their own little joke-filled town.

So wander here with a gleeful heart,
Where laughter and nature never part.
In winding woods, the fun runs deep,
Where every secret's yours to keep.

The Enigma of the Ebon Shadows

In shadows deep where laughter hints,
A mystery stirs; it laughs and glints.
A midnight owl with a knowing hoot,
Shares tales of creatures who play pursuit.

Ebon shadows stretch and sway,
Mischief cradled in night's ballet.
The glowworms giggle, glinting bright,
Leading the way through sheer delight.

A playful ghost with a silly wink,
Makes even the bravest of hearts rethink.
"Don't take life too seriously, dear,"
He whispers softly, spreading cheer.

In shadows' embrace, the night unfolds,
With laughter ringing, brave and bold.
The enigma of joy blooms in fright,
In ebon shadows, all feels right.

The Nature of Nightfall Nuances

When twilight drapes its velvet veil,
The squirrels gather, start their tale.
With acorns caught in fuzzy cheeks,
They plot their heists, exchange their tweaks.

A raccoon's eyes, like lanterns gleam,
While fireflies join in this night's dream.
They flicker tales of pizza loot,
As owls hoot 'bout their best fruit loot.

The moon winks down, a cheeky ghost,
As shadows dance, they laugh the most.
In whispered squeaks and rustling leaves,
Each critter's secret, none believes.

Nightfall's tunes are hilarious notes,
Rambunctious creatures clad in coats.
With jests exchanged beneath the stars,
The woodland's stage, with no bizarre.

Sundrops on Swaggering Saplings

Little trees with pomp and flair,
Strut their stuff in the sunlit air.
Each leaf a dancer, green with pride,
In the breezy bash, they cannot hide.

Sunbeams tickle, laughter flows,
As branches twist in playful throes.
Nature's comedians, so sprightly and spry,
With every rustle, a joke to fly.

Buds nod like wise guys from a show,
While petals blush and steal the glow.
In floral frocks, they can't be tamed,
With all their antics, they're never shamed.

Swinging in breezes, they trade their cheer,
With every gust, they dance without fear.
In this spruced-up jesting parade,
Mirthful saplings hardly evade.

Chronicles of the Crescendoing Canopy

High above, the branches bicker,
Who's the tallest, who's the quicker?
While leaves gossip in breezy chat,
One shouts, 'I'm the verdant brat!'

A woodpecker joins with a knock,
To settle scores like a ticking clock.
He drums a tune, tapping with glee,
'It's all about rhythm, can't you see?'

Beneath the boughs, a squirrel scampers,
Ninja moves, oh, look at his pamper!
Swings from limbs like a tree-bound star,
He knows no bounds, he'll go too far.

With laughter echoing the sky,
Woeful leaves say, 'oh my, oh my!'
In this leafy leadership play,
The canopy thrives, come what may!

Epiphanies Amidst Entwined Elders

Old trees mumble in knobby tones,
Their barked wisdom, scattered bones.
Twisting branches share their quirks,
In merry snickers, the history lurks.

'What's the secret to longevity?'
One whispers low, with pure levity.
'It's all about stretching, don't you know?'
While mossy old gnomes nodding slow.

A breeze slips through with a cheeky grin,
Rustling tales of where they've been.
Their laughter echoes, sipping dew,
In storiesfresh, all bright and new.

So here they stand, proud and wise,
With every rustle, a new surprise.
Nature's jesters, forever keen,
In their woven tales of evergreen.

Chronicles of the Forgotten Forest

In the woods where whispers play,
The trees gossip night and day.
Squirrels wear tiny hats, quite bold,
Trading nuts for tales retold.

A beaver builds a bridge to fame,
While raccoons join in the game.
They dance to the moon's silver light,
Making merry all through the night.

The owl hoots out a crazy joke,
While branches sway and trees provoke.
A frog jumps in with laughter loud,
Joining the antics of the crowd.

In this haven of whimsy bright,
Every creature shares delight.
Nature's comedy finds its way,
In the forest's amusing play.

Fluttering Thoughts in Foliage

Amidst the leaves, the butterflies tease,
With paths that twist like tangled breeze.
A bee stings laughter into the air,
While rabbits frolic without a care.

The flowers chuckle, their petals bright,
As bees buzz jokes in morning light.
A ladybug disputes a leaf's claim,
While petals giggle, playing their game.

The breeze hums tunes, a playful sound,
Tickling every critter on the ground.
They intermingle in a joyful spree,
Nature's laughter, light and free.

In foliage deep, my thoughts take flight,
Hatch a smile in the golden light.
Fluttering whims among the trees,
Life's a jest that aims to please.

Reveries of the Rooted Ones

In the soil where roots are deep,
The trees share secrets that they keep.
They chuckle softly in the shade,
As acorns bounce, a sprightly parade.

Old branches bend with tales of yore,
While wildflowers laugh from the forest floor.
A worm jokes on its squiggly route,
Amidst the laughter, a verdant shout.

Mushrooms sprout and join the mirth,
Jesting about their humble birth.
With every rustle, they play their part,
Reveries sprout from a living heart.

Together they dream of sunshine bright,
Alive with antics by day and night.
The rooted ones in their leafy spree,
Share in the jest of this grand jubilee.

The Poetics of Thicket and Thorn

In thickets thick where thorns combine,
The critters scheme and craft their design.
A porcupine dons a prickly hat,
While hedgehogs giggle at a sleeping cat.

The bushes sway, a leafy stage,
Hosting a play for the woodland wage.
Splendid brambles sing out in tune,
With laughter that floats beneath the moon.

A lizard slips with a wink and a grin,
Teasing the shadows, let the fun begin!
Each rustle and whisper, a punchline shared,
In the thicket, no moment is spared.

The poetics of nature, a whimsical tale,
Where laughter echoes, and joys prevail.
Through thorns and brambles, life's charm is spun,
In Nature's theater, there's always fun.

Reflections from a Mossy Hollow

In the hollow where moss giggles,
Frogs wear crowns made of twigs.
Squirrels play chess with acorns,
While the ants march in dance jigs.

The mushrooms hold court for the bugs,
Whispering secrets in fungal tone.
A snail's a poet in a shell,
Yet his verses are low on their own.

Who needs a bard when trees can laugh,
With branches that wave like raucous gents?
Nature's a jester in green and brown,
Spilling punchlines with leafy intents.

So, come take a peek at the fun,
In the mossy depths, where humor's unbound.
The whimsy is thick, like berry stains,
And echoes of laughter are all around.

Beneath the Gnarled Canopy

Beneath the canopy so tangled,
Gnomes tell tales of questionable sense.
With hats that sway like topsy turvy,
Their wisdom's as clear as a dense fence.

Leaves gossip among the branches,
Chasing each other in fray and swirl.
A raccoon wearing spectacles,
Reads a guide on how to twirl.

The forest floor's a stage of jest,
With beetles performing their stunt shows.
Bats hang out as night-time critics,
Jotting reviews with tiny prose.

Hilarity blooms in this green parade,
Where laughter's a leaf that doesn't decay.
Join the festivities, don't be late,
Under the gnarled, giggling sway.

The Poetry of Petals and Pine

In the woods where petals prattle,
The pine trees snicker with glee.
A daffodil's rhyme is very odd,
As it claims it's the best, you see!

Butterflies start a poetry slam,
Winged verses float like soft clouds.
And daisies, with their upturned heads,
Cheer wildly, like raucous crowds.

But alert! The crows critique with flair,
Claiming art is but a chirp away.
Yet no one listens to their caws,
As laughter drowns their words of gray.

So let's toast to petals and pines,
In this garden where humor reigns supreme.
Beneath the sun's warm, witty gaze,
Nature's art is the ultimate dream.

Heartbeats Among the Ferns

Amidst the ferns where shadows dance,
Lies a heartbeat ticking sideways.
With critters plotting a strange romance,
Undercover in leafy hallways.

The earthworms host a comedy night,
Jokes about digging and dirt in between.
While spiders weave tales in spite,
Of getting old and becoming unseen.

Mice compete in acrobat leaps,
Chasing each other through roots and vines.
Even the mushrooms join the fun,
With caps that tell tales crossed with pines.

So venture forth, join the vibe,
Where heartbeats echo in the vibrant green.
Among the ferns, the laughter thrives,
It's nature's secret show, always unseen.

Whispers of the Wildwood

In a forest where the squirrels play,
The trees gossip in a charming way.
Breeze tickles leaves, laughter on high,
While mushrooms debate who's the fun guy.

A raccoon tried to tell a joke,
But ended up in a puffy cloak.
The owls rolled their eyes, feathers fluffed bright,
As a chipmunk danced in the pale moonlight.

Beneath the ferns, secrets abound,
With every rustle, new tales are found.
The wildflowers giggle, a colorful scene,
As pine cones ponder what it all means.

So if you wander through this whimsic wood,
Just laugh at the trees, oh yes, you should!
For nature has her own witty rhymes,
Making merry with the rhythms of time.

Echoes of Ancient Treetops

High up where the breezes snooze,
The treetops gossip, sharing their views.
A squirrel interrupts, with a flick and a flare,
Claiming he knows why the birds don't care.

A wise old owl hoots, standing tall,
"Why don't we reason? Let's hold a ball!"
The leaves all rustle, a woodland affair,
Where raccoons serve snacks without a care.

A bashful deer shows off her dance,
While rabbits leap about, taking a chance.
With every spin, the branches sway,
As the forest chuckles, come what may.

Yet whispers linger, "Who's got the moves?"
With rain dropping down, they all improve.
In echoes of laughter, the treetops sway,
Dancing together in their own funny way.

The Philosopher's Grove

In a glade where the ponderers sit,
The mushrooms debate the meaning of wit.
One claims to know, "It's really quite clear,"
While the daisies just giggle, "Oh, come over here!"

A turtle in glasses weighs in with delight,
"Time's just a snail, moving slow as night."
But the frogs croak loud, "You've missed the great quest!

It's all about fun, not the mind's heavy jest!"

So gathered they, these thinkers profound,
In a circle of wisdom, where laughter is found.
Each thought wove a tapestry of jest,
As the stumps shook with joy, quite truly impressed.

When night falls, the stars shine bright,
In the grove where they ponder the mysteries of light.
But amid the silence, a giggle floats high,
For even the wisest can't dodge a sly pie!

Bark and Blossom Reflections

Under branches, where shadows creep,
The blossoms converse, secrets to keep.
A fervent debate on who's best in bloom,
While the bark chuckles, "Just give it some room!"

"Are we charming or just a pretty charade?
In the grand scheme, does beauty evade?"
The roses wink, "We have the best smell,"
While dandelions shout, "We're doing quite well!"

The willow sighs, "Each has its own flair,
Whether in sunlight or caught in the air."
As the petals shimmer with laughter and cheer,
The bees hum a tune that we all can hear.

So in this garden, each bloom has a role,
With bark and blossoms finessing the whole.
When you wander here, don't take it too hard,
For life is a garden, oh, sweetly absurd!

Enigmas of the Everchanging Season

When spring arrives, the bunnies giggle,
They paint their fur with pollen wiggles.
In summer, sunflowers wear shades of gold,
While ants march on, so brave, so bold.

Fall brings pumpkins, round and plump,
They dance with squirrels, a lively thump.
Winter sends snowflakes in a swirl,
They dress the trees in a frosty whirl.

What's next, you ask, in nature's game?
A squirrel in winter, thinking it's fame!
With acorns stacked in a tower tall,
He claims he's King of the Forest Hall.

So dear friends, embrace the jest,
In seasons' whims, we're all quite blessed.
With laughter tucked in each petal and leaf,
Let's savor the folly, and dance with relief.

The Lure of Leafy Labyrinths

In forest paths where shadows play,
A raccoon sings, "Hey, let's stray!"
Through tangled greens, we twist and turn,
While lively crows teach us how to yearn.

A hedgehog rolls, so round and spry,
Chasing butterflies that flutter by.
What's this confusion, can we retrace?
Oh look, a snail's now in the race!

Down mossy lanes, the laughter's free,
As critters play hide-and-seek with glee.
The branches high whisper secrets sweet,
While frogs croak truths in a rhythmic beat.

We wander lost, but all in fun,
In leafy realms, we laugh and run.
So here's to journeys, strange but grand,
Where quirk and magic stroll hand in hand.

Dreams of the Decomposing Earth

In the garden where the veggies sigh,
A cabbage dreams of flying high.
Tomatoes giggle, ripe and red,
While whispered tales of lettuce spread.

A worm waltzes in the soil so dark,
Claiming its fame in a squiggly park.
Carrots below blush, "We're so fine!"
While radishes boast, "We're roots divine!"

When autumn comes, leaves take a bow,
The earth hums softly, "Let's compost now!"
With worms delighting in a leafy feast,
When it's all over, no one's the least.

For in decay, there's laughter spun,
As life returns, we've barely begun.
In dreams of growth, let's all be wise,
For the quirky squabbles are the best surprise!

Harmonies of Hidden Haven

In a nook where shadows twist and twine,
Crickets play tunes with zest and shine.
Fireflies dance like stars in gloom,
Spreading giggles in the secret room.

A hedgehog hums a soothing song,
While a wise old owl plays along.
They serenade the sleepy night,
With hiccups of fun, oh what a sight!

The breeze whispers softly through the trees,
Tickling the leaves like giggly peas.
Mushrooms sway, in a silly jig,
Declaring, "Life's better when you're big!"

So gather round, in this hidden space,
Listen close to nature's embrace.
For laughter blooms where hearts are brave,
In this haven, the good times save.

Wandering Words of the Wildwood

In the forest where trees hold court,
A squirrel in a tie plays the sport.
He challenges the owl to a riddle spree,
But the owl just hoots, 'Can you fly like me?'

The rabbit talks fast, can't find his pace,
While the beetle checks time, but it's lost in space.
'What's for dinner?' the fox slyly calls,
'Only the best, if you're dodging the falls!'

Leaves gossip softly, but who can they trust?
With branches so crooked, it's just a must.
A chipmunk claims he's famous in France,
But his only applause is from the plants' dance!

The Language of Lichen and Moss

Amidst the stones where the lichen dreams,
A turtle shouts, 'Life is bursting at seams!'
He speaks to the moss, so soft and so green,
'What's your secret? You know how to glean!'

The moss replies, 'Just stick to your roots,
And find your friends among the boots.
In silence, we flourish, with giggles so meek,
Join the dance of the shadows, let laughter speak!'

A snail glides past with bravado untrue,
'I'm the speedster of all, just wait 'til I do!'
While a nearby rock rolls its ancient eyes,
Whispering tales of surprise and goodbyes.

Tangents of the Twisting Trunks

Two trees twist up in a spiraled chat,
'You call that a trunk? I've seen better fat!'
The birch scoffs lightly, 'Your bark's not so fine,
Not like my stripes, so sleek and divine!'

A worm down below, with a keen sense of style,
Grins up at the trunks, 'Stay tangled awhile!
Your arguments bore me, just branches and knots,
But tell me of your leaves, or I'll connect dots!'

As shadows stretch long, they start a new game,
Playing 'Who's the tallest?' with laughter untame.
'Truth is I'm wise, but you're catching up fast,'
Said the elder, as the sun sank low at last.

Verbal Whirlwinds in the Verdant

In the greens where words swirl like leaves,
A fox spins tales, of nets and thievery he weaves.
'Catch me if you can!' he calls to the hare,
But she just rolls eyes, ignoring the flair.

The ferns disagree, shaking fronds left and right,
'Your tales are as grand as a shadow at night!'
A robin warbles, perched high on a branch,
'Let's form a band, a woodland romance!'

The raccoon joins in, with a scrap of old news,
'I've sipped from the creek, and am down to my shoes.
Let's push our stories, till the stars are all out,
In this wild wood, laughter's what it's about!'

Breezes Carrying Forgotten Tales

Whispers of the wind dance bright,
Tickling leaves in silly flight.
Stories hidden in playful breeze,
Tales of squirrels and jumbled keys.

Clouds giggle as they drift away,
Bumbling by in a soft ballet.
They drop a rain-drop, splat on my nose,
Oh, how nature's humor flows!

Dandelions laugh in joyful throng,
As butterflies flutter around all wrong.
Each petal spins a merry jest,
Nature teasing, she's quite the pest!

Rabbits leap with a comic flair,
While grasshoppers sing without a care.
A dance of critters, silly and spry,
Under the gaze of a watchful sky.

Pauses in a Green Reverie

In the shade, I lounge and sigh,
A squirrel stares with a raised eye.
The moss below has a cozy grin,
Inviting me to just dive in.

A butterfly struggles, flapping fast,
Trying to sip from a flower's cast.
The petals laugh, it's quite a scene,
As it tumbles like a clown, so keen!

Sunbeams tickle the sneaky breeze,
As I ponder life with doomed ease.
Fish in the pond swim round and round,
Playing hide and seek, what a sound!

The trees hold court, gossiping leaves,
While chubby ants march, full of thieves.
They cart away crumbs, quite the show,
In this green reverie, spirits glow.

Nature's Tantrum and Tranquility

Oh, what a fuss the clouds do make,
Huffing and puffing, for goodness' sake.
They spill their rain with a mighty roar,
While flowers giggle on the wet floor.

Thunder grumbles, yet fails to scare,
As puddles form with such flair.
A rainbow slips out, bright and bold,
Nature's temper, a sight to behold!

Then calm comes sneaking, soft as a sigh,
A bunny hops by, with a curious eye.
The world's a stage for creatures and blooms,
Mixing joy in the remnants of booms.

Crickets chirp their happy tune,
Beneath the watch of a silvery moon.
Nature's tantrums bring laughs in waves,
Tranquility follows, all mischief saves!

The Wisdom of Twisted Branches

A gnarled tree gives winks of wit,
As squirrels chatter, not a moment to sit.
With branches bent in quirky arcs,
It speaks of secrets and silly sparks.

Leaves flutter down in a lopsided race,
Teasing the wind in a leafy embrace.
Crows caw loudly, wearing a crown,
In this twisted realm, no one wears a frown!

The roots wiggle with ancient tales,
Of mischievous sprites and fairy trails.
Beneath the bark, laughter rolls deep,
Nature's wisdom is intertwined, we leap.

So come, dear friend, take a look around,
At the twisted branches, where joy is found.
In this woodland of whimsy, we learn and play,
Life's a riddle, in the funniest way!

Secrets of the Sylvan Silence

In woods where giggles softly dwell,
A squirrel's secret, who can tell?
Whispers dance on leafy breeze,
While owls chuckle from high trees.

Mushrooms wear their silly hats,
Snoring frogs make strange chitchats.
A rabbit's gossip, quick and light,
Tickles the curious moonlit night.

Among the branches, shadows sprite,
Conspiring beneath the twilight.
Nature's jesters play the tune,
Of laughing leaves and merry rune.

Remember, in this forest grand,
Laughter weaves through every strand.
Each rustling twig and rustle free,
Hides a joke, just wait and see!

Symphonies of the Sunlit Glade

In glades where sunlight reigns supreme,
The daisies plot a dancing scheme.
Butterflies wear their best attire,
While beetles gossip, never tire.

A breeze huffs, a gust climbs high,
Tickling leaves as it saunters by.
Grasshoppers join in joyful leaps,
While silly shadows play in heaps.

The brook hums tunes of wily glee,
Giving secrets to the bee.
Frolicking ants parade in line,
Their tiny antics set to rhyme.

In this carnival of the light,
Every corner brings delight.
Laughter weaves through the glade's embrace,
A sunlit smile on nature's face.

Riddles of Rain and Reflection

When raindrops fall with a gentle grin,
    Puddles form a shiny skin.
With every splatter, a gleeful cheer,
    As clouds crack jokes, oh so near.

The worms rejoice, they wriggle free,
    Waltzing 'neath a willow tree.
Chirping crickets play their song,
    Under a sky where all belong.

Raindrops play their musical notes,
    Tickling toes of little boats.
Reflections laugh, a wobbly sight,
While sunbeams dance away the night.

Nature's riddles, a playful spree,
    Every drop a mystery.
With giggles masked by gentle rain,
The world whispers back, "Try again!"

The Lament of the Lost Sapling

A sapling stood, with dreams alight,
Yearning to stretch, to touch the height.
But vines entwined its little frame,
Chanting softly, "What's your name?"

The breeze would tease, "You're much too small!
Forget your dreams, just watch us all!"
The sapling giggled, "I'll stand tall,
One day, I'll surprise you all!"

It knows the sun will share a spark,
To light the path, dispel the dark.
With roots so strong and heart so bold,
It dreams of stories to be told.

So let it dance, though may seem odd,
In garden's realm, it's still a prod.
For every whisper, every sway,
Holds laughter for a brighter day!

Notes from the Nectar-Nurtured Nook

In the garden where giggles grow,
Bees wear shoes, just so you know.
The daisies gossip about the sun,
While the tomatoes challenge each other to run.

A squirrel performs its finest dance,
To impress the woeful glance.
With acorns as its audience, they cheer,
And the blossoms giggle, 'Oh dear!'

The butterflies play tag in the breeze,
While ants debate who carries with ease.
Somewhere a gopher has popped its head,
Yelling, 'Last one home is a moldy bread!'

Laughter ripples through leafy lanes,
As nature tells jokes without any chains.
At the nook, the fun's never done,
Just snickers and giggles under the sun.

Dialogues of Dappled Dreams

Two frogs in a puddle discuss the weather,
One claims it's too hot, the other says 'Together!'
They croak out tunes with a rhythmic hop,
While a dragonfly's chorus goes on nonstop.

Beneath the shady boughs, a wise owl hoots,
Arguing with a crow about fashionable boots.
'Your flapping is boring!' the crow caws back,
'At least my style doesn't go off track!'

A flower chimes in, 'Oh please, be neat!
Your bickering's worse than my wilting defeat.'
But they all burst into laughter instead of fighting,
For friendship is best with a touch of delighting.

In the dappled dreams of sunset's gleam,
Anything possible, just follow the theme.
As whispers of joy lift high above,
Nature's vibrant dialogue speaks of love.

Ponderings from the Petal-Paved Path

Pondering life with a daffodil flair,
'Why do squirrels always steal my hair?'
A petal sighed, 'Oh, such petty strife,
Can we not ponder the good things in life?'

Butterflies flutter in bemusing chatter,
Debating whose wings are the best at patter.
They travel the world flapping in sync,
While a wandering bee stops for a drink.

The sunflowers affirm, 'It's all just a game,
We bloom in the wild, but none is to blame.'
With roots in the soil, they share stories grand,
Of adventurous days in wonderland.

Together they laugh on the petal-paved way,
In a world where fun rules the day.
For life's but a carnival, brightly adorned,
With flowers and friends, all joyfully scorned!

Fables of Ferns and Fronds

Fern and Frond had a curious chat,
Debating the merits of being quite fat.
'I'm oh-so-slim,' said Frond with a grin,
'But I bend and sway, where's your spin?'

'You may be flexible, but round's my crown!'
Said Fern with a swagger, 'When tossed, I won't drown!'
They laughed till they tumbled, roots in a knot,
'Perhaps our shapes matter not!'

A ladybug joined with a giggly haste,
'Why bother with shapes when we have such taste?'
With spots and stripes, they all shared a giggle,
As raindrops began to play their own wiggle.

Fables unrelated, now oddly entwined,
In nature's narrative, true friends you'll find.
Where laughter blooms and blossoms sway,
Fern and Frond find joy in every day.

Verses of the Veiled Vines

In a tangle, they twist and they twine,
A ballet of leaves, oh how they shine!
They gossip of roots and the rain's sweet kiss,
While the sun laughs above, a blissful abyss.

Worms wear top hats, the bugs waltz too,
A party for critters, a vine-covered view.
They toast with dew drops, the morning's best cheer,
While the daisies roll deep in their giggles near.

A squirrel in a suit juggles acorns with flair,
While the laughing grass whispers, "Come dance if you dare!"
The vines sway and sway as they capture delight,
In this leafy world, everything's just right.

A chorus of nature, hilariously bright,
Where every small creature joins in for a flight.
In this tangled ball, where the funny unwinds,
The joy of the verdant forever entwines.

The Pulse of the Pine-Scented Breeze

Oh, the wind carries jokes from tree to tree,
Whispering secrets of sheer jubilee.
The needles all snicker, the branches all sway,
With a rhythm so merry it brightens the day.

Pines wear their cologne, oh so fragrant and bold,
While the maples just giggle at stories retold.
The whole forest chuckles, it's quite a grand scene,
As the breeze tosses laughter like confetti of green.

The acorns are clapping, their caps perched real proud,
While nearby, the ferns form an uproarious crowd.
A dance on the wind, an entertaining tease,
All thanks to the pulse of that pine-scented breeze.

Leaves rustle with glee, under skies ever clear,
Where even the shadows come forth to appear.
Nature's sharp humor, oh what a delight,
With every breath taken, the world's just so bright!

Chronicles of the Creaking Canopy

Hear the tales of the trees with a creak and a crack,
Old branches recounting the joys of their track.
The bark's full of stories, a wonderful lore,
Each rustle a giggle, each sway an encore.

The owls hoot in rhythm, conducting the night,
While the fireflies twinkle, oh what a sight!
With a flick of their wings, they spin whimsy and grace,
In this leaf-laden theater, we revel, we trace.

The squirrels are jesters, with antics so sly,
Their peppy little dances make everyone sigh.
The canopy chuckles, a riotous show,
As the stars twinkle down, encouraging the flow.

A symphony grows, with each creak of the wood,
In the charm of the night, where mischief has stood.
These chronicles sung, in the moon's tender light,
Where everything's funny, and laughter takes flight.

The Essence of Elms and Oaks

Elms whisper secrets in a melodic tone,
While oaks shake their branches, in icy winds blown.
Laughter rings out, from the roots to the tops,
As the branches do jiggles and dance, never stops.

In this lively grove, winks and giggles abound,
A festival blossoms, with merriment found.
The crickets take charge, the grasshoppers strive,
In this riotous revel of nature alive.

The shade holds a party, with shadows that sway,
As the flowers serenade the warm sunny day.
Petals pop champagne, in this comedy show,
Where even the soil hums a jovial flow.

So come join the laughter, in this grand evergreen,
Where jokes are like pollen, all flying and keen.
The essence of elms, of oaks standing tall,
In the heart of the grove, where the funny is all!

Musings Beneath the Maple Canopy

Under the branches, shadows play,
Where squirrels plot their nutty day.
A raccoon's laugh, a chipmunk's cheer,
I swear they're plotting, oh dear, oh dear!

With each rustle, the leaves conspire,
To make a jest, light-hearted fire.
A dance of whispers, giggles fly,
Nature's jesters, oh me, oh my!

The bees gossip over the sweetened bloom,
While ants are busy planning their doom.
On the ground, I shuffle my feet,
In this comedy, nature's heartbeat.

So here I sit, my heart aflutter,
As foliage chuckles, a leafy utter.
With laughter around, it's hard to be blue,
In this lively theater, ah, how we grew!

Echoes from the Elder Grove

In the hushed embrace of ancient trees,
Whispers carry on the teasing breeze.
Subject of jest, the owl winks sly,
As rabbits bet on who'll hop high.

The foliage chuckles, a rustling sound,
While shadows dance on the cold, hard ground.
Oh, what a spectacle under the sun,
Nature's humor, a comedy run!

Raccoons plunder the picnic spread,
While old man tree shakes his leafy head.
"Just leave them some crumbs," he bellows with glee,
"Tomorrow we feast—just wait and see!"

In this grove of laughter, I find my place,
Where even the breezes have a funny face.
With echoes of giggles that never cease,
I savor the whimsy, the joy, the peace.

Reflections in a Rustling Meadow

In the meadow bright, the daisies converse,
While butterflies argue, a colorful verse.
The grass hums softly, a comedic tune,
As clouds roll by, wearing a cartoon!

With whispers of daisies tickling the air,
A ladybug claims her throne with flair.
And the crickets croon their nightly song,
In this vibrant opera, we all belong.

The sun sets low, bringing a chuckle,
As fireflies flicker, a glowing buckle.
Each laugh carries high, over hill and glen,
In this meadow of mirth, again and again.

Watching stars peek, in a funny disguise,
With twinkling laughter painted on skies.
I dance with the meadows, a carefree swirl,
In this enchanting laughter, life's joyful twirl!

Conversations with the Dancing Leaves

Around the boughs, the breezes tease,
Leaves chatter sweetly, a playful breeze.
"Did you hear what autumn said?"
The maple laughed and flipped her head.

A waltz of whispers, a joke untold,
With every flutter, new tales unfold.
The oak just chuckles, all wise and grand,
"Life's but a prank, isn't it grand?"

With each passing gust, a new quirk revealed,
In this leafy theater, laughter's appeal.
The verdict is clear, as they sway to and fro,
To the rhythm of giggles, a verdant show!

So let's raise our voices, join in the mirth,
In the heart of the forest, there's always rebirth.
For every leaf's laugh, under skies so blue,
Reminds us of joy, old or new.

Soundwaves of the Sweet-Scented Soil

In the garden where the gophers play,
Frogs serenade with a croaky ballet.
Worms wiggle and twist in their muddy delight,
While daisies gossip under the moonlight.

Bees zoom around with their buzzing chatter,
Picking up gossip like it's the latest matter.
A sunbeam slips on a buttercup hat,
It's the fashion show, and oh, how they prattle!

Funky plants wiggle, doing the twist,
While dandelions laugh at being missed.
Earthworms dance in their squishy attire,
A muddy jig that never tires.

In this sweet-scented realm, oh what a laugh,
Even the carrots join in for the half!
So, prance with the petals and waltz with the weeds,
The soil sings tunes that tickle the seeds.

The Harmonies of Honeyed Breezes

Whispers float by on a lilting breeze,
Flavored with laughter from the buzzing bees.
A butterfly fumbles; it can't take a cue,
Tripping on petals, poetry in view.

Mints leaf through notes of a fresh-lemon serenade,
Spices join in with a spicy charade.
Jasmine chuckles in the warm sunny glow,
While the daisies argue on how to steal the show.

Thyme tells a story, basil rolls its eyes,
Every herb here wears a fragrant disguise.
Suddenly a gust sends them all in a spin,
Spaghetti and sauce, the dance will begin!

In this dish of delight, oh what a fare,
Even the garlic can't help but share.
So let's toast to the blooms and the giggles they bring,
A tasty adventure, let the laughter sing.

Prophecies of Petals and Pollen

Petals whisper secrets, swirling about,
Sneaky predictions, without a doubt.
Roses claim they'll soar on a kite,
While violets giggle, planning a flight.

Dandelions blow wishes till they're spent,
Swaying on dreams that are never quite bent.
Pollen sprinkles tales on a soft, sunny day,
Spreading laughter in its own sunny way.

Lavenders gossip 'neath a fluffy white cloud,
While sunflowers beam, oh so proud.
"What's next?" they muse, as the wind starts to swell,
"More antics, more fun? Time will tell!"

So here's to the blooms on this whimsical ride,
Where every petal has laughter inside.
They'll giggle and chortle, a flowery spree,
In the garden of chaos, we all are free.

Odes to Obscured Sunbeams

Sunbeams peek through in a game of hide and seek,
Trying to shine on the flowers, so chic.
But clouds play tricks, chuckling loudly,
As daisies dance with petals so proud and rowdy.

On a patch of clovers, mischief abounds,
Every shadow sings with the softest of sounds.
As ladybugs flee from their tickling toes,
Nature's own circus, and everybody knows.

Butterflies giggle, flaunting their hues,
While squirrels debate which acorn to choose.
The breeze bursts in like a musical jest,
Causing daisies to whirl, it's a spontaneous fest!

So wrap up the sunbeams in laughter and fun,
Each obscured ray dances before the day's done.
In the court of the flowers, all life is a play,
And every mischief adds color to the day.

www.ingramcontent.com/pod-product-compliance
Lightning Source LLC
Chambersburg PA
CBHW071819160426
43209CB00003B/136